Successful Nonprofits Build Supercharged Boards

Successful Nonprofits Build Supercharged Boards

Dolph Ward Goldenburg

This Publication is designed to provide accurate and authoritative information in regard to the subject matter covered. It is sold with the understanding that neither the publisher nor the author is engaged in rendering legal, accounting, or other professional service. If legal advice or other assistance is required, the services of a competent professional person should be sought.

ISBN: 0692376054
ISBN 13: 9780692376058
Library of Congress Control Number: 2015901494
The Goldenburg Group, LLC, Atlanta, GA

How to Use This Book

Does your organization experience issues with board members

- Not attending board meetings?
- Not participating on committees in a meaningful way?
- Interacting in ways that disrupt meetings?
- Focusing on operational issues instead of policy and oversight?
- Failing to make an annual contribution?
- Not fundraising effectively?

If lack of board engagement and effectiveness is holding your organization back, this book will provide you a comprehensive system to supercharge your board. Written for busy nonprofit professionals and board members, this book is intentionally short. Each chapter is packed with helpful tools, without the verbose fluff common in too many professional books.

Using this system will increase your board's engagement, commitment, and productivity. By following each step, in order, your organization will emerge from the process with a supercharged board.

Some readers will pick up this book and think "I want to start with the chapter on recruitment," or "I want to just use the chapter on committees." These readers will gain valuable information to improve their recruitment strategy or committee structure. However, their boards will still lack key skill sets and won't perform at the highest possible level.

To gain the most from this book, you should first read it from start to finish. Once you understand the entire system, you can then return to Step 1 and get to work supercharging your board.

STEP 1

Conduct A Board Evaluation

The first step in supercharging your board is to conduct a comprehensive board evaluation. It is important to assess the performance of the board as a whole and of individual members.

Since the evaluation lays the groundwork for supercharging your board, it is important to conduct it thoughtfully and thoroughly.

The board evaluation will:

- Assess board member knowledge of the organization's mission, programs, goals, and challenges.
- Assess board participation with regard to governance, regulatory compliance, fundraising, and financial oversight.
- Determine board strengths, as well as gaps in knowledge and skills among board members.
- Determine areas on which members have general consensus and areas that require further deliberation.
- Identify high performing and underperforming members.
- Help underperforming board members realize they are not meeting expectations.
- Identify training topics that will benefit the entire board.
- Establish training needs for individual members.

Depending on the size of the board, the evaluation process will require one to two months and include the following stages:

Stage One: Drafting an evaluation tool
Stage Two: Interviewing or surveying board members
Stage Three: Analyzing responses
Stage Four: Analyzing other information as necessary, such as board giving reports or attendance records
Stage Five: Developing a report
Stage Six: Presenting this report to the entire board

Drafting the evaluation tool

While this chapter ends with a sample evaluation tool, it is best to customize a tool for your organization that incorporates the board's existing policies and procedures. If using an independent consultant to conduct the evaluation, your consultant will be instrumental in developing a strong evaluation tool.

Regardless of whether an organization customizes the sample or creates its own evaluation tool from scratch, the evaluation should solicit feedback regarding each member's knowledge of the organization, participation, and fundraising. It should also give each member the opportunity to comment on the organization's strengths and challenges, as well as on the evaluation tool itself.

The document should primarily offer open-ended questions, allowing for an open, conversational discussion. Such questions are more likely to elicit thorough, honest feedback from board members and provide an opportunity for greater depth.

Conducting the evaluation

While a board can independently work through the other stages of the supercharging process, it is ideal to hire an independent consultant to conduct the evaluation. The consultant will approach the evaluation with greater objectivity and will have experience working with a number of other boards of directors. Additionally, board members are more likely to share candidly with a consultant without the fear of offending the interviewer.

The organization should structure a process for selecting a consultant that obtains buy-in from the board and executive director. One option is for the executive committee and director to interview prospective consultants together, inviting consultants to share their proposed evaluation tools and processes.

Once the executive committee and executive director have selected a candidate, they should present their nominee to the board for confirmation. The motion to approve should also make continued board service contingent on participating in the evaluation and follow up board retreat if such a stipulation is consistent with the organization's bylaws.

If cost is an issue, a consultant can often lower fees by conducting phone interviews or using an online survey. However, an online format will provide significantly less information.

It is critically important that every board member participate in an individual interview, so you should select a consultant who can offer flexible times and locations for conducting them.

The organization should allocate no more than four to six weeks to complete all interviews to ensure the process continues to move forward.

Usually at least one board member will be "too busy" for an interview. This board member is likely too busy to continue board service. The board chair should call that board member and ask that they either make time to participate in the evaluation or step down from the board. Should the busy board member be unwilling to do either, the board should vote to remove that board member at its next meeting. Once again, all board action must be consistent with organizational bylaws.

Cost of hiring a consultant

Since the cost of hiring a consultant depends on a number of variables, the best way to estimate costs is to ask a few respected local consultants. Some variables that impact cost include:

Level of experience: Someone who has conducted evaluations for fifty boards of directors will charge considerably more than someone who has conducted only one.

Size of your board: Since the bulk of the work is in surveying board members and analyzing responses, board size will directly affect cost. Evaluating a ten-member board will take significantly less time than evaluating a board with twenty-five members.

Method of surveying your board: The three most common methods of surveying the board are face-to-face, phone, and written surveys. Face to face interviews are the most time consuming and, therefore, the most expensive. Of course, in-person interviews also generate the most valuable feedback.

Method of analyzing data: If the evaluation document is composed of primarily open-ended questions, compiling data from the responses will take more time and cost more. While responses to multiple-choice questions are easier to analyze, they will also provide more limited, less meaningful information.

Travel requirements: If the consultant must travel from another region, the organization will pay more to cover travel expenses. If your organization is in a rural area with few qualified consultants, you may wish to have the consultant work remotely (for example conducting telephone interviews) and travel only to deliver the final report to the board.

Final deliverables: Both the organization and the consultant should be clear about the final deliverables, as this will impact the amount of work and consulting fees. Specifically, does the board want to receive the final report with recommended steps and then follow-up on each of the steps independently? Alternately, does the board want the consultant's help in structuring board trainings, board recruitment, and board orientation?

The consultant may charge a higher fee to conduct the evaluation as a stand-alone assignment than as part of a larger contract. Clarifying the full scope of work up front may allow the board to realize potential savings over retaining a consultant piecemeal.

Organizations without funds to hire a consultant

Before deciding that your organization cannot afford to hire a consultant, brainstorm some ways to raise the necessary funds. These might include:

- Asking a current program funder for a one-time grant
- Asking the board to donate or fundraise the amount needed to conduct a board evaluation
- Asking the local community foundation about an organizational development grant to fund the evaluation

If attempts to raise the funds do not succeed, organizations can conduct an internal evaluation with a few modifications. Most important, you should use a written or online survey instead of the conversational interview. This will make it easier for all board members to offer candid responses.

If not using a consultant, the board should also appoint a committee to conduct the evaluation and produce a report. Committee members should have at least three additional hours per week to commit to the project: one half hour to an hour for weekly phone meetings and the remaining time for evaluation tasks. The committee's most important role is to keep the evaluation moving forward.

Analyzing the data

After collecting significant data, the consultant or evaluation committee will look for trends. In order to do this, much of the qualitative data will need to be translated into quantifiable data.

As an example, while members might provide twelve different responses to a question about strengthening the board orientation process, the evaluators may find three trends in the responses. Perhaps they identify the need for (a) a structured half-day orientation; (b) a mentorship program that pairs a stellar, experienced board member with each new member; and, (c) the need to teach board members how to read financial statements.

The evaluators will also review responses to identify general consensus among board members. If, for example, eleven of twelve board members agree there is an expectation that all board members make a personal gift, then the follow-up report will note that this consensus exists and focus attention on the need to reach agreement regarding the minimum amount of each personal gift.

The final evaluation report should include conclusions and next steps for the board in each of the following key areas:

- Board member knowledge of the organization's mission, programs, goals, and challenges
- Governance, financial oversight and regulatory compliance
- Board strengths, as well as gaps in knowledge and skills among board members
- Fundraising
- Areas on which board members have general consensus and areas that require further deliberation and decision
- Training the entire board should receive
- Training individual board members should receive (without naming those board members individually)

Presenting and using the report

Once the report is compiled, you should plan a full or half-day retreat for the consultant or evaluation committee to review it with the board.

In addition to reviewing the report, the retreat should allow time for the board, with guidance from the consultant, to develop a plan of action that addresses several key areas:

- Board member responsibilities and expectations
- Rules of Engagement
- Fundraising
- Recruitment
- Orientation
- Training
- Committees
- Meetings

- Staff Roles
- Relationship with the ED/CEO

Each of these areas is discussed in depth in a later chapter.

Next steps

After completing the board evaluation, you can proceed without additional services from a consultant if board members are fully committed to following all the steps outlined in this book.

If your organization lacks the resources to engage a consultant for the remainder of this process, you must have an energized committee dedicated to moving the process forward. Members of your committee will likely volunteer an additional three to four hours per week for several months in order to fully supercharge the board.

For organizations planning to conduct the board evaluation without a consultant, a sample written board evaluation survey follows on the next several pages.

Sample Board Evaluation Tool (written or online)

Thank you for serving on the XYZ board. Please set aside 45 to 60 minutes to complete this board evaluation survey. Since this survey is designed to solicit information about the governing body that will guide recruitment, orientation, training, and expectations of board members, please complete the survey based on your own understanding and thoughts without consulting internet or staff resources. When the survey asks for a specific number, please provide your best estimate. Please use as much space as necessary to write your answer and the line will expand as you write.

Most importantly, this survey is not a test. It will not be "graded" and only aggregate data will be shared with the board.

Board Member's Name: _____

Year Joined: _____

Please provide some demographic information:

Gender: ❑ Male ❑ Female

Race: ❑ African American ❑ Asian/Pacific Islander

❑ Caucasian ❑ Other:

Ethnicity: ❑ Latino ❑ Non-Latino

Date of Birth:

The first few questions assess the board's knowledge of the organization.
In your own words, describe the mission of the organization:

What are the key programs or services of the organization?

What are the key goals of the organization?

How well has the organization performed in achieving those goals?

The next few questions assess the board's role in governance.
When did the board last evaluate the executive director?

What role(s) did you play in the evaluation?

What committee(s) do you serve on?

How often do(es) your committee(s) meet?

What role do you play on the committee(s)?

Please check all of the financial documents distributed and discussed at the last board meeting you attended:
- ☐ Profit and loss statement/statement of functional expenses
- ☐ Balance sheet/statement of financial position
- ☐ Accounts payable and receivable reports

Based on the financial documents distributed at the last board meeting you attended, please answer the following questions:

Does the organization currently have budget surplus or deficit?
    ☐ Surplus   ☐ Deficit

Did the fund balance increase or decrease from the same period last year?
    ☐ Increase   ☐ Decrease

The current fund balance represents approximately how many days of operating?

The current cash balance represents approximately how many days of operating?

Who gave the financial report at the last board meeting?
- ☐ Treasurer   ☐ Assistant Treasurer
- ☐ CFO   ☐ Executive Director   ☐ Other:

The next few questions assess board recruitment, orientation and training.
Before joining the board, how did you find out about the organization?

Please describe the recruitment and nominations process when you joined:

Why did you choose to join this board instead of another organization with a similar mission?

Please describe the orientation you received as a new board member:

How well did this orientation prepare you to be an effective board member:
- ☐ I felt completely prepared
- ☐ I felt well prepared but had several knowledge gaps
- ☐ I felt somewhat unprepared
- ☐ I felt completely unprepared

If you did not feel completely prepared, what specific knowledge gaps did you experience?

How would you recommend strengthening the orientation process?

How would you recommend strengthening the orientation process?

Please describe the training opportunities offered to board members in the past twelve months:

In which of these opportunities did you participate?

Were you able to participate in as many training opportunities as you wanted in the last twelve months?

If not, what prevented your participation?
- ☐ The training was not offered
- ☐ Training session time or location was not convenient
- ☐ I was too busy to add anything else to my schedule
- ☐ Other:

What board training would you like to receive?

What type of training best suits your schedule and learning style?
- ☐ Weekday trainings offered at the local nonprofit center
- ☐ Weekend trainings developed for and held at our organization
- ☐ Thirty-minute trainings held before each board meeting
- ☐ Online training ☐ Other:

The next few questions address the board's skills and skills gaps.

Below is a list of skills that most nonprofit boards require. Please review this list and indicate skills you can or do provide, as well as skills you feel the board is currently missing.

Area of Expertise	I have this skill	No Board Member Currently Has
Legal		
Accounting		
Programs		
Fundraising		
Marketing		
Media Relations		
Board Governance		
Advocacy		
Client Population		

What other skills do you bring to the board?

If you have skills that this board under-utilizes, please describe them:

What do you feel is currently the board's greatest strength?

What do you feel is currently the board's greatest weakness?

The following questions assess the board's role in strategic planning.
When was the last strategic plan approved?

If the plan has been reviewed or revised, please indicate when:

What do you feel is the most important goal in the strategic plan?

What do you feel is the greatest challenge facing the board in the coming 12 months?

What do you feel is the greatest challenge facing the organization in the coming 12 months?

What strengths or assets does the organization have that can help overcome these challenges?

The following questions assess the board's engagement in fundraising.
Is there an expectation that each board member make an annual financial gift?

If yes, what is the minimum amount a board member is expected to give?

Approximately how much did you give in the last twelve months? (Please include all donations you made personally, but do not include your employer's gifts, funds you raised, or in-kind gifts.)

Approximately how much money did you fundraise for the organization?

Please describe how you raised the funds (include tickets sold, solicitations made, etc.):

The following questions determine how the board functions.
In general, do board meetings start on time?
　　　□ Always　　　□ Usually　　　□ Occasionally　　　□ Never
If you indicated Occasionally or Never, what are the most frequent reasons for meetings to start late?

In general, do board meetings end on time?
　　　□ Always　　　□ Usually　　　□ Occasionally　　　□ Never
If you indicated Occasionally or Never, what are the most frequent reasons for meetings to end late?

In general, approximately how long do most board meetings last?
　　　□ <1 hour　　　□ 1-2 hours　　　□ 2-3 hours　　　□ 3+ hours

In general do you feel the length of meetings are:
　　　□ Just right　　　□ Too short　　　□ Too long

How would you describe board member interaction at board meetings (check all that apply)?

☐ Everyone offers his or her opinion.

☐ Most board members actively participate.

☐ Everyone doesn't offer opinions at every meeting, but everyone feels comfortable sharing their opinions.

☐ One or two board members rarely or never speak.

☐ One or two board members speak too much.

The final set of questions gauge the organization's regulatory compliance.
I completed a conflict of interest disclosure document:

☐ In the last 12 months

☐ When joining the board but not since

☐ I have never completed a conflict of interest disclosure.

I received and reviewed the independent auditor's report and management letter in the last twelve months:

☐ Yes   ☐ No

I received and reviewed the organization's most recent Form 990:

☐ before it was submitted to the IRS

☐ after it was submitted to the IRS

☐ I did not receive the most recent Form 990.

I received and reviewed a copy of the organization's charitable registration with the Secretary of State within the last 12 months:

☐ Yes   ☐ No

I received and reviewed a copy of the organization's directors and officers insurance within the last 12 months:

☐ Yes   ☐ No

Finally, what recommendations do you have for improving this evaluation document in the future?

STEP 2

Set and Enforce Expectations

The importance of setting expectations

Everyone lives with a set of expectations, whether at work, within a family, or in the community. In some settings, we may have no need for documenting and affirming the expectations. For example, nearly everyone in a family probably agrees that the last person going to bed should turn off the lights.

On the other hand, setting, communicating, and enforcing expectations is essential in our workplaces and in the community, because humans typically seek the norm. That is, most people will conform to what is average among their peers. If your board has two high-performing members, eight mediocre members, and two low-performers, a new board member is likely to be only as involved as the mediocre members. More important, individuals with the potential to be truly high performers are unlikely even to consider joining a board with only two other high performers.

For this reason, boards of directors need to develop, approve, and enforce minimum expectations for all board members.

Reviewing board evaluation data is the first step in identifying expectations that board members already share, as well as expectations the board needs to set. Specifically, evaluation data is likely to indicate whether there is agreement on the following:

- Meeting attendance and participation
- Fulfillment of fiduciary responsibility
- Conflicts of interest

- Committee participation
- Personal financial gifts
- Fundraising requirements

The system outlined in this book will help the board develop consensus on expectations, approve the expectations as policy, and enforce them.

Expectations: Board meeting attendance and participation

Attendance and participation in board meetings is crucial for a functioning board and is essential for board members to fulfill their individual fiduciary responsibilities. After all, how can a member knowledgeably vote at meetings if he or she does not attend a majority of those meetings?

Setting expectations for attendance and participation starts at the executive committee level. The executive committee should first review the organization's by-laws to determine whether this important legal document outlines the attendance requirements and the consequences if someone does not meet them.

If the by-laws address attendance requirements, the executive committee should determine whether those requirements and consequences are still acceptable. If they are, then the chair should remind board members of the attendance requirements at the next meeting and document expectations as described later in this chapter.

If the by-laws do not fully address desired attendance requirements, the executive committee must deliberate and make a recommendation to the full board about the number of meetings a board member must attend each year. Additionally, the executive committee's recommendation (or existing by-laws) should address members who attend only part of the meeting, attend meetings remotely or provide a proxy.

While each board will set its own expectations and must abide by (or change) their by-laws, recommended rules are as follow:

- Boards meeting monthly require attending ten meetings per year; boards meeting bi-monthly, five meetings per year; boards meeting quarterly, four meetings per year.

- Members must attend at least 80% of any meeting for attendance to count.
- If the organization has the capacity to host a conference call or video link, attending a meeting remotely is acceptable as long as the board member has a work or health related reason that prevents attending in person.
- A member who votes by giving proxy to another (if by-laws allow) is not considered to have attended the meeting.

Expectations: Fulfillment of fiduciary responsibility

Since every board member has a fiduciary responsibility, your organization should outline specific expectations regarding the exercise of prudent fiscal oversight. Since legal requirements may vary by state, it is important to consult an attorney in crafting your own board expectations regarding this matter.

At a minimum, board members must meet the following expectations:

- Have a basic ability to read and understand financial statements, including balance sheets, income and expense statements, and statements of accounts receivable and payable.
- Review financial statements before every meeting and ask for an explanation of items they do not understand or that they believe to be unusual, incorrect, or outside of acceptable ranges.
- Review the annual independent auditor's report and audited financial statements, and vote to accept or reject the auditor's report. This process usually includes a meeting with the auditor to discuss any findings or issues of concern.
- Review IRS form 990 and raise any concerns before the organization submits it to the IRS.
- Review and vote on salary ranges for all positions. (Note: the board should not vote on the specific salary of any employee other than the executive director.)
- Vote on the compensation for the executive director or CEO and ensure it is comparable to similarly sized organizations in the same region.

- Deliberate and vote on board motions in a manner that protects the organization's assets while remaining consistent with the organization's mission and complying with all regulations and laws.
- Avoid all conflicts of interest unless they have been expressly disclosed in writing and the board has properly voted to allow the conflict.

If a conflict of interest is disclosed and allowed by the board, members with a conflict should recuse themselves from any deliberation and from all votes related to the matter in conflict.

At least annually, every board member should certify in writing whether they have conflicts of interest. When unsure whether a conflict exists, board members should disclose the potential conflict of interest.

Expectations: Committee participation

Since committees do most of the work of a supercharged board, your board needs to have a common expectation about active committee service. An upcoming chapter discusses the important work that committees undertake, so this section will focus entirely on expectations of committee service.

Serving on a committee enables board members to really connect with a specific aspect of the organization. While board meetings expose all members to a breadth of information about the organization, committee service ensures that members become intimately familiar with programs, finances, human resource challenges, and other aspects of the organization's operations.

In setting expectations regarding committee service, the board must determine the minimum number of committees each board member is required to join.

The size of the board will, of course, impact the number of committees on which members are required to serve. A five-member board, for example, may need each member to serve on several committees, while a board with fifteen members may require each member to serve on only a single committee.

Just as with board meeting participation, expectations regarding committee work should also provide a definition of active participation. This will include attendance at a specified percentage of meetings and may also address those who arrive late or leave early.

Expectations: A personal financial gift

All boards should expect that each member will make a personal financial gift every year. There are three reasons that 100% board giving is critical:

- Foundation and corporate funders review the percentage of board members who made a financial contribution in the past 12 months. They view less than 100% giving as indicating a weak and disengaged board. As a result, organizations with board members who don't contribute financially are significantly less likely to obtain grants.
- Board members should be actively involved in fundraising, but they cannot ask others to give without having made a personal donation themselves.
- Board members' sense of ownership always increases after making a financial investment in the organization.

If your board does not already require an annual personal gift from each board member, officers need to guide the board in reaching agreement on this expectation. Such guidance is critical because conversations about money can be quite difficult and uncomfortable. As with other difficult conversations, it is best to discuss this matter directly and openly.

If any officer of the Board has not made a gift in the past twelve months, the first step is to get financial buy-in from each officer. This may mean the board president meets with officers individually to discuss the importance of 100% board giving and to solicit a personal gift.

Once each officer has made a personal financial gift, the executive committee can determine an appropriate policy recommendation for board approval. Boards typically set the minimum board giving in one of the following ways:

As a minimum dollar amount. The stated dollar amount could be as low as one dollar or as high as thousands of dollars. This method provides real clarity about the minimum acceptable gift, but has two primary drawbacks. If the minimum amount is set too high, potentially good board members may be unable to serve. If set too low, some board members with greater ability to give will still give the minimum acceptable gift.

As a top philanthropic priority. Many organizations ask board members to place the organization among their top three philanthropic priorities. This approach recognizes that board members may have other philanthropic commitments, while helping guide their decision about the amount to give relative to their other gifts.

As an undefined commitment, such as stating "everyone must make a gift at least once a year." This is the least effective policy, as it gives no guidance to board members.

The Executive Committee should present this clearly defined board giving expectation to the entire board. After developing an expectation supported by a majority of members, the board should pass a motion requiring that each board member make an annual contribution to remain in good standing.

Expectations: Fundraising and relationship management

While fundraising and relationship management strategies are discussed in an upcoming chapter, the board should establish basic expectations for board members' involvement in fund development. This process should begin in the development or fundraising committee. If your board does not have a functioning development committee, then the executive committee should start the process of forming a policy while also establishing a development committee.

In recommending an appropriate minimum amount for each board member to raise, the development committee should discuss the fundraising efforts they are individually willing to undertake and existing fundraising opportunities available to board members.

Additionally, the development and executive committees should determine the appropriate number of relationships for each board member to manage. The chapter on fundraising will provide greater depth on this topic, but essentially each board member should help cultivate relationships with a small number of individuals, foundations, and/or corporations. This can be as simple as keeping them up-to-date on the organization's progress and personally inviting them to important events.

The committee should present to the Board a formal proposal for board fundraising expectations that includes:

- The annual minimum each board member should raise
- The minimum number of relationships each board member should manage and cultivate
- A statement that continued board service requires meeting this expectation

Documenting expectations for board service

The process of developing expectations is finalized with a one-page document that outlines the basic expectations of board service and the manner in which they are enforced. Each current board member should acknowledge they have received the document, and it should become an integral part of the recruitment and orientation of new board members.

A sample board expectation document is provided at the end of this chapter.

Enforcing expectations for board service

Your board must have a mechanism for enforcing expectations. If none exists, the executive committee should propose one for board approval. Some boards elect to remove under-performing board members, while others offer the member a leave of absence until they are able to meet those expectations.

Regardless of how your board chooses to enforce expectations, it is critical that those who fail to meet expectations be removed immediately from active board service. For this reason, the enforcement mechanism must be intrinsic and occur without any deliberation or vote. Too many boards create an enforcement mechanism that states a board member "may be removed" for not meeting expectations. However, these boards rarely vote to remove under-performing board members, which then undermines the expectation for all board members.

When considering possible enforcement mechanisms, the executive committee should ensure their proposal is consistent with the organization's by-laws. If the recommendation is not consistent with the by-laws, the proposal must also recommend appropriate revisions to the by-laws.

Board Expectations Report

Current As of September 30, 2014
Confidential – For Executive Committee Only

	Jane Doe	Jon Johnson	Jane Smith	Jim Williams
# of board meetings attended YTD	8 of 9	7 of 9	9 of 9	8 of 9
# of committee meetings attended YTD	9 of 9	7 of 8	9 of 9	8 of 9
$ given YTD	$1,100	$550	$575	$2,250
$ raised YTD	$4,300	$100	$7,500	$2,300
Conflict of interest disclosure submitted?	Y	Y	Y	Y

Once expectations are approved, documented, and acknowledged, the executive committee is charged with ensuring that board members meet them. Each executive committee meeting should review a dashboard indicating each board member's status, which should require less than ten minutes to review and discuss.

After reviewing this report, the executive committee assigns its members to contact those at risk of not meeting expectations.

If, for example, the board requires attendance at 10 of 12 monthly board meetings, an executive committee member would reach out to Jon Johnson and encourage his attendance at the last three meetings of the year because he has already reached the maximum allowable number of absences. In this conversation, Jon may indicate that his job will prevent him from attending meetings for the next three months and either ask for a leave of absence or offer to resign from the board.

The personal communication from an executive committee member is essential because an under-performing board member should be given every opportunity to meet expectations.

Additionally, every board member receives a personal status report showing his or her own summary of attendance, donations, fundraising success, and conflict of interest compliance. These individual reports are typically prepared and sent by a staff member before each meeting.

Placing a board member on leave of absence

If the enforcement mechanism includes an automatic leave of absence for an under-performing board member, the process for placing a member on a leave of absence can be a positive experience for everyone.

The officer assigned to communicate with an under-performing member should do so with the utmost respect and compassion. The conversation may start by asking what is preventing the board member from meeting the expectation. Most often, the board member will cite unexpected work or family issues. Perhaps the member is now doing the job of two people due to a workforce reduction, or perhaps he or she has recently begun caring for a sick parent or child.

At this point in the conversation, the board officer needs to communicate that the member brings great skills and assets to the board but the organization needs every member's full participation, citing the specific expectation that is not being met.

Then the board officer can communicate, again with compassion, that the member will be placed on leave of absence from the board until the work or family situation allows the member to return to full service. During that time, the member will be relieved of all board responsibilities to concentrate on the other issue(s) that are preventing full board commitment.

The board officer should offer to follow-up in three months. The officer should also let the board member know to expect a letter from the board president confirming the leave of absence.

When leaves of absence are used, it is essential that the board follow-up with the member who is on leave. First, the board president must send the follow-up letter referenced above. Additionally, it is important that a board officer actually follow- up at the established time to ask whether the member is able to return to full board service. This follow-through demonstrates that the organization sincerely values the person's previous service and that board representative's compassion is genuine.

At the three-month follow-up, most people on a leave of absence will either express an ability to return to full board service or offer to resign, having come to the realization that they will be unable to meet the expectations of board service.

Terminating an under-performing board member

If the enforcement mechanism is automatic termination, the executive committee should once again communicate this with the utmost compassion.

A member of the executive committee should personally speak with any board members being terminated to inform them of their removal from the board.

In this conversation the officer should (a) thank the member for previous service and point to a specific contribution the board member made; (b) explain that the decision was not personal and remind the member that termination is automatic based on the enforcement mechanism; and (c) explore other ways the person can be involved in the organization.

Sample Board Expectations Document

To promote the mission of XYZ organization, the board has established the following expectations of each board member.

Attendance:

❖ Attend at least 8 of the 10 board meetings (no meeting is held in August or December). Attendance is defined as being present for at least 75% of the meeting.

Committees:

❖ Participate in at least one committee and attend at least 75% of the committee meetings.

Fundraising

❖ Make a personal annual financial contribution to XYZ organization that is personally significant.

❖ Raise at least $1,000 annually for XYZ organization through ticket sales, personal solicitations, and sponsorships.

❖ Manage at least three relationships with current, prior, or potential donors.

Oversight:

❖ Review financial statements before each meeting; review the annual audit and IRS Form 990 in a timely manner; disclose all conflicts of interest in writing; and deliberate and vote on board motions in a manner that protects the organization's assets while remaining consistent with the organization's mission and complying with all regulations and laws.

Board members unable to meet these expectations will be automatically placed on a leave of absence until they are able to meet them.

_____   _____

Board Member Signature   Date

STEP 3
Define Rules of Engagement

The board should establish "rules of engagement" that delineate how individual members interact with each other, the board as a whole, and the staff. Each board will want to develop their own rules of engagement but should consider the following:

Board Member Authority. Unless expressly granted by board action (vote), no member has the authority to speak on behalf of the board or the organization, nor to enter into contracts for the organization.

Civil Discourse. Board members will discuss all issues civilly, speaking in a straightforward, respectful manner to everyone.

Committees. Since most board work begins at the committee level, members should address policy recommendations to the appropriate committee, rather than raising these for the first time at a board meeting.

Confidentiality. Board members must keep information obtained through board and committee service in the strictest confidence. If a member must disclose confidential information to meet legal or ethical obligations, that member will inform the board and executive director in writing of such disclosure.

Naysaying. Every board member has the right to disagree, but a board cannot function effectively if one member expresses disagreement in every discussion. Someone who plays the role of naysayer becomes an obstacle for the entire board and also loses the ability to credibly express dissent. Eventually, a naysayer becomes an impediment to getting the board's work done.

Operations. Individual board members do not have the authority to oversee day-to-day operations of the organization.

Policy. Individual board members do not have the authority to set policy on behalf of the organization.

Preparation for Meetings. Board members agree to prepare for meetings by reviewing all materials prior to the meeting. This also requires that the organization send all meeting materials at least one week before each scheduled meeting.

STEP 4

Revitalize Committees

A supercharged board does most of its work through committees. Various committees are responsible for fiscal oversight, policy development, strategic program oversight, fundraising planning, and advocacy. Each of these areas requires in-depth research, discussion and oversight that the board as a whole simply does not have time to do. Additionally, if every board member had to become an expert in each of these areas, serving on a board would essentially become a full time job.

Strong committees also streamline the work of the board. For example, five committees that each meet for ninety minutes will provide more than seven hours of deliberation. Without committees, this board would have unreasonably long meetings and be too rushed to deliberate issues fully.

For this reason, committees bring recommendations to the board for action, and the board should rarely vote on a motion that has not been considered by a committee. This chapter will describe some of the most common committees, their role in the organization, and a typical twelve-month calendar for each.

Executive committee

The executive committee is traditionally composed of the board officers and is responsible for oversight of the board. The president-elect and immediate past president often serve on the Executive Committee to provide leadership continuity, and the executive director participates in committee meetings as well.

The executive committee is responsible for the following tasks:

- Setting the board meeting agenda
- Ensuring board members meet expectations and following up with those who do not
- Ensuring the board meets its legal obligations
- Ensuring each committee is functioning and meeting goals

Executive committees typically meet two weeks before each board meeting to review committee reports and set the agenda for the upcoming meeting. In addition to this ongoing work, the committee's annual workflow may occur like this:

Month 1: New executive committee meets for the first time. Reviews the strategic plan to determine goals for the current year and annual board calendar (to include board meetings, retreats, orientation, and any special events already scheduled). The calendar will likely require input from other committees.

Month 2: Ensure board members have submitted fundraising plans and conflict of interest disclosures. Create a follow-up plan for those who have not yet submitted these documents. Plan and execute review of executive director evaluation, ensuring the whole board has the opportunity to provide input.

Month 3: Begin planning the annual board retreat. Report on any board members who have not submitted their annual documents and determine whether the committee should recommend a leave of absence for those members. Discuss results of executive director evaluation with the board and then the executive director.

Month 4: Finalize plans for the annual retreat.

Month 6: Conduct a mid-year review of strategic plan progress and goals. Plan a report to the board.

Month 8: Identify board-level mission critical tasks for the final four months of the year. Meet with committee chairs to discuss as necessary.

Month 10: Plan for executive committee transitions, to include a wrap-up report and recommendations for the next year's executive committee.

Finance committee

The Finance Committee is chaired by the board treasurer and should include at least two other members with expertise in reading and understanding financial statements. Every board must have a Finance Committee to meet its fiduciary responsibility.

Staff is responsible for sending unaudited financial statements to the Finance Committee at least a few days prior to each meeting, and the highest level accounting/bookkeeping staff member should be available at the meeting to answer questions. Especially in small and medium sized nonprofits, the executive director attends Finance Committee meetings as well.

The Finance Committee is responsible for fiscal oversight and for providing sufficient information to the board so all members can fulfill their fiduciary responsibility. At a minimum, the Finance Committee should:

- Review financial statements including balance sheets, income and expense statements, statements of accounts receivable and payable, and cash flow projections.
- Report on the financial statements at each board meeting and answer any questions.
- Ensure the completion of an independent audit.
- Ensure compliance with IRS regulations.
- Oversee the annual budgeting process and conduct a mid-year budget review.
- Present the budget and mid-year budget adjustments to the board for approval.

Finance Committees typically meet at least two weeks before each board meeting and review financial statements at every meeting. In addition to this monthly task, the monthly workflow usually follows a pattern similar to that outlined below:

Month 1: Create plan for engaging the auditor, which may include a motion either to engage the most recent auditor or to begin a bid process for selecting a new auditor.

Month 2: Review financials from the prior fiscal year and approve a motion to engage the selected auditor.

Month 3: Review insurance policies of the organization. At a minimum these should include general liability, professional liability/errors and omissions, employment practices liability, workers compensation, and directors and officers coverage. Depending on the scope, programs, and facilities of a nonprofit, additional types of insurance may be needed.

Determine whether current insurance coverage is sufficient or a change in carriers or types of coverage is needed. If your organization decides to issue a request for bids for new carriers, the committee should recommend whether to use a broker or negotiate directly with insurance companies.

Month 4: Review audit draft and meet with the auditor. Discuss any audit findings and approve any required remediation. Some important questions to ask an auditor include:

- Can you describe any issues that should concern us?
- What issues exist concerning internal controls? Are these characterized as material weaknesses or significant deficiencies? How do you recommend we rectify them?
- Is this an A-133 Audit that includes specialized regulatory compliance tests for organizations receiving more than $150,000 in Federal funding? If it is, can you describe any regulatory compliance issues that were uncovered?
- Are there any operating procedures you identified as inefficient or unnecessary?
- What was your relationship like with staff while conducting the audit?
- How do our internal controls and accounting practices compare to similar nonprofit organizations?
- Should we anticipate issues with the IRS or our Federal funders? If so, how can we prepare for these issues?

Plan to present the audit at the next board meeting, and ask that the auditor attend as well. The auditor's report should be distributed with the pre-board meeting packet, and the board should vote at this meeting to approve or reject the audited financial statement and independent auditor's report.

Month 5: Review the annual return for tax exempt organizations (IRS Form 990) in detail, and ensure the information is accurate. In addition to ensuring accurate financial reporting on the 990, pay special attention to the questions regarding the organization's governing body and management: Part VI, Sections A, B, and C (as of the time this text was written).

Month 6: Review income and expense projections for the next six months and prepare any recommended budget changes for board approval.

Month 7: Begin drafting the next fiscal year's budget with significant involvement from staff leadership and other committee chairs. The lead staff accountant or bookkeeper should assist by updating and maintaining the budget spreadsheet and providing cost estimates. The fundraising committee and development staff (or executive director) can provide income projections, and each committee should have the opportunity to request and explain any new proposed expenditures.

Month 8: Continue drafting budget.

Month 9: Prepare final budget and present at the next board meeting.

Month 10: Perform a six-month follow up with the executive director to ensure continued compliance with any new accounting practices that were adopted to address issues found in the audit.

Month 11: Prepare wrap-up report and recommendations for the next year's Finance Committee. Review finance manual to ensure the organization's compliance. Recommend revisions to the manual for board approval.

Program specific committee(s)

A board member who is a subject matter expert in the field typically chairs a program committee. This committee usually includes board members, program staff leadership, and respected community members. Most small organizations will have only one program committee, while more complex organizations may need a committee for each program or group of related programs.

A program committee is typically responsible for:

- Reviewing program data (number of clients served and quantifiable impact) and reporting it to the board.
- Governance-level program recommendations to the board including significant policy changes, development of new programs, or expansion or dramatic change to existing programs.

Smaller organizations may need to rely on program committees to perform some of the functions typically completed by staff or consultants at larger organizations. This may include measuring outcomes and analyzing raw data.

Program committees should be careful to make governance-level program recommendations only and not attempt to manage programs. A few examples of operational decisions that do not rise to the level of governance include:

- Whether a program will operate from 8:00 AM - 4:00 PM or from 7:00 AM - 3:00 PM.
- Whether a specific candidate is hired to fill a staff position.
- Whether a program will terminate a relationship with an underperforming sister agency.
- Which database application is used to track client data.

At each committee meeting, program committees should review output and outcome data, being certain to discuss any issues that specific programs are encountering. In addition to this periodic activity, the annual workflow for a program committee might follow this outline:

Month 1: Review program data from the prior year, and goals for the new year. Determine committee goals (as distinct from program goals) for the year and the annual meeting schedule.

Month 5: Discuss potential program expansions and changes for the next fiscal year. Assign committee members to partner with the appropriate staff who will research the cost and impact on program outcomes and mission of proposed changes

Month 6: Formulate recommendations for finance committee consideration in the budgeting purposes.

Month 9: Recommend prospective board members to the Nominating Committee. While the Executive Committee and Finance Committee are composed entirely of board members, the Program Committee is in a unique position to have a knowledge of program volunteers and former clients who may make good board members.

Month 10: Develop program overview presentation for next year's board orientation.

Fundraising committee

The fundraising committee, in close partnership with development staff, provides governance-level oversight of all fundraising for the agency and drives volunteer fundraising for the organization. Together, the committee and development staff determine the strategy for the annual campaign and special events.

Larger organizations with endowment or capital campaigns have separate committees for these purposes. In addition, some larger organizations with diverse funding sources may have multiple fundraising committees or subcommittees for different donor groups and events.

The primary fundraising committee is composed of board members and community volunteers who have a record of successfully soliciting donations and hosting special events as volunteers. Development staff, or the executive director in the case of smaller nonprofits, is an integral part of this committee.

The Development Committee reviews fundraising results compared to projections each month and may have the following additional workflow activities:

Month 1: Review fundraising results from prior years and reaffirm goals for current year. Confirm fundraising calendar, to include dates of special events as well as the start and end dates of the annual campaign. Finalize campaign and event themes. Discuss recruitment strategies for any subcommittees.

Month 2: Review the fundraising portion of each board member's individual fundraising plan and ensure there is a mechanism for including them in the appropriate volunteer fundraising efforts. Report back on recruiting subcommittee members. Review the plan for the spring campaign, being certain to have a mechanism for engaging board members and volunteers as appropriate.

Month 3: Check in regarding the annual campaign and reports from special events subcommittees or staff.

Month 4: Check in regarding annual campaign and reports from special events committees. Identify final steps necessary to ensure underperforming campaigns reach goals. These steps might include a last call for donations, a call to arms for additional volunteers to conduct solicitations, or additional supports that volunteers need to be successful.

Month 5: Provide Finance Committee with realistic fundraising projections for the following fiscal year, along with a justification for the projections.

Month 6: Review results of the annual campaign, discuss changes necessary for end-of-fiscal-year campaign, and plan accordingly. Review reports from special event subcommittees. Discuss anticipated fundraising results for current year and report to finance committee for budgeting purposes.

Month 8: Finalize and launch the end-of-fiscal-year campaign. Review reports from special event subcommittees.

Month 9: Discuss progress of end-of-year campaign.

Month 10: Discuss any changes necessary to meet end-of-year campaign goals. Discuss fundraising plan for the next fiscal year.

Month 11: Debrief with key volunteers on results of fall campaign. Determine and document what was successful and recommend changes in campaign strategies for next year. Work closely with staff who are finalizing the fundraising plan for next fiscal year, and discuss fundraising presentation for next year's board orientation.

Month 12: Review campaign results and make any changes necessary in volunteer assignments. With staff guidance, identify fifteen to twenty additional solicitations that must occur before the end of the fiscal year (may be more for larger organizations), and assign each solicitation to a volunteer/staff pairing. Finalize the presentation for the next year's board orientation.

Human resources committee

Larger organizations typically have a human resources committee that makes recommendations to the board regarding employment policies, pay scales, and benefits. The committee also serves as a resource to the executive director for difficult human resource issues.

The committee is typically chaired by a board member with professional expertise in human resources, and usually has only board members and the executive director as members.

The typical workflow of this committee includes the following:

Month 1: Create annual meeting schedule and work plan for the year. Assign committee member tasks based on the work plan. Assign committee members to research equitable pay scales from similar organizations in the region.

Month 3: Review pay scale research to ensure compensation remains competitive with other nonprofit organizations. Recommended pay scale changes should be reported to the finance committee if immediate salary adjustments are needed. The board must also approve recommended changes.

Month 6: Review employee benefits and assign committee members to research any proposed changes. The additional costs or savings that would result from these changes should be reported to the finance committee for planning purposes.

Month 9: Discuss any human resource policy changes that are required. Employee situations that arose in the prior year will often bring such required policy changes to light. The committee should consult with an attorney specializing in employment law to develop or review proposed policy changes. This policy review should be conducted annually, and all changes will need to be approved by the full board.

Month 12: Ensure the organization has completed annual evaluations on all staff. If it has not, report this to the executive committee to be included in the next executive director evaluation.

Nominating committee

The nominating committee is perhaps the most important board committee because it determines the organization's future volunteer leaders.

Some organizations add board members throughout the year, but boards function more efficiently when the nominating committee conducts one annual board recruitment campaign and orients all new board members as a group.

The workflow of the nominating committee includes:

Month 1: Review skills and connections of current board members, whose terms are not expiring, and determine any gaps. Additionally, determine the number of available board positions including current vacancies and members with terms that end in the next twelve months. Assign committee members to discuss the possibility of another term with those board members whose terms expire and are eligible to continue.

Month 2: Prepare a report indicating which members with expiring terms wish to continue serving. Update the skills analysis and then structure a board recruitment campaign (see the chapter on recruitment). Determine process for orienting new board members, including the date of the orientation session.

Month 3: Launch recruitment campaign. Committee members report on conversations with prospective board members.

Month 4: Recruitment campaign ends. Review applications and select candidates to interview. During interview, ask candidates to "save the date" for the orientation. Finalize orientation process, including agenda and materials for the orientation session.

Month 5: Interview prospective board members, check references, and make position appointment recommendations to the board. Finalize the orientation process for new board members.

Month 6: Follow up with all candidates, including those not appointed to the board. The most effective organizations link candidates who were not appointed to the board to other committees for service. Host new board member orientation session, and follow up as necessary to ensure new board members continue the orientation process.

Staff liaison

Each committee should have a staff liaison who is the highest-level staff member for that function. As examples, the executive director should serve as the liaison to the executive committee, and the CFO should serve as the liaison to the finance committee.

The staff liaison's role is to:

- Assist the committee chair in developing an agenda for each meeting
- Arrange all logistics of committee meetings
- Send meeting agenda and meeting packets to committee members before the meeting
- Take minutes at each meeting and send them to the chair for review and approval

Jurisdiction and scope of committees

Committees are vital in the life of any organization, and they are responsible for much of a board's work. A committee, however, has the authority only to make recommendations to the whole board. Ultimately, the board is responsible for approving the recommendations and ensuring they are implemented.

Once the board has approved a policy, its implementation rests solely with the staff. While the board as a whole must hold the executive director or CEO accountable for implementing policy, staff are solely responsible for running programs and daily operations.

Additionally, no board or committee is ever responsible for directly managing a program, implementing policy decisions, managing staff, or making employment and termination decisions. These remain key staff functions, and committees attempting to take such actions cause role confusion for all staff, the board, and the clients served. This role confusion undermines the organization's ability to provide programs and meet its mission.

STEP 5

Make Meetings Effective

These guidelines for effective meetings apply to board meetings and committee meetings alike. If followed, they will ensure more effective governing bodies with laser-like focus on the most important tasks.

Meeting schedule

The board and each committee should publish a meeting schedule the first month of the year. The schedule should include the time, date, and location of each meeting, as well as the details for any teleconference attendance options. Once published and distributed, it should not change. For this reason, holiday calendars and leadership's personal travel schedules should be considered when creating the annual meeting schedule.

Agenda and meeting packets

No meeting should ever occur without a written agenda. Agendas are essential to ensuring efficient and effective meetings, but many organizations meet without them or waste the first ten minutes of a meeting creating an agenda.

An agenda provides structure to the meeting and allows participants to prepare for a productive meeting. Most important, however, a meeting agenda requires board or committee leaders to define the purpose and goals of the meeting. A good agenda also assigns a time limit for each item, which ensures each matter is acted on and provides the chair with a mechanism to table any issue that requires additional work or discussion beyond the allocated time.

For this reason, the person who chairs a meeting is ultimately responsible for developing the agenda and ensuring it is followed. Having said this, the staff liaison is an integral partner in developing and distributing the agenda, and a staff liaison may need to remind a busy chair of the need to develop an agenda. Effective chairs will respond to a staff member's initial reminder, since failure to respond will require that staff needlessly spend time sending multiple emails, texts, and voicemails.

One effective way to develop the board meeting agenda is to ask committee chairs whether they have a report for the board. In assigning times for the agenda status update reports may be kept to less than three minutes per committee, while reports requiring board discussion or vote should be allotted significantly more time (usually ten to twenty minutes).

The meeting chair should also ask each person placing an item on the agenda for a written report that members can review prior to the meeting. These reports, along with the agenda and YTD financials, are sent as part of the pre-meeting packet at least one week before the meeting itself.

Typically, assembling and disseminating the meeting packet is a staff member's responsibility, but smaller nonprofits may need a board or committee secretary to manage this process.

The agenda is also a good way to gently remind board members of upcoming events, fundraising opportunities, board deadlines, and other important upcoming dates.

Reports at board meetings

Committee chairs, not the executive director or committee staff liaisons, should present reports at each board meeting.

Board Meeting Agenda
October 15, 2014
6:00 PM – 7:30 PM

Attendance Options:

In person:	Phone Conference:
347 Main Street, 2nd floor	Conference Line: 1-800-555-5555
Atlanta, GA 30303	Conference code: 123456#

Agenda:

I. Approval of minutes – 3 minutes (vote)

II. Executive Committee Report: 2015 officer election – 15 minutes (vote)

III. Finance Committee Report
    YTD Financials – 7 minutes (vote)
    FY 2015 budget – 20 minutes (vote)

IV. Program Committee Report
    Update on program outcomes - 3 minutes
    Client testimonial - 10 minutes

V. Fundraising Committee Report: Update on Fall Campaign - 3 minutes

VI. HR Committee Report: Changes to PTO policy – 15 minutes (vote)

VII. Executive Director Report – 5 minutes

Reminders and Announcements:
➢ Next board meeting is November 19
➢ Major donor brunch and annual meeting is Saturday December 6
➢ Please complete your fall campaign solicitations before the November
   board meeting

Generally speaking, the report should provide a high level overview and outline any board action that needs to occur.

During each report, the board should avoid doing the work of a committee. It may choose to send a motion back to a committee for further work or consideration, suggesting the committee consider specific changes or recommendations. Once tabled, the item should return to the board for consideration only after the committee has completed its work on the motion.

Meeting minutes

A board member or staff person should have the responsibility for taking minutes at each meeting. To ensure consistency in how minutes are recorded, this responsibility should remain with the same person for an entire year.

Keeping succinct minutes that state attendance, status report topics, motions and votes will ensure that the actual business of the organization is fully documented, without detailing unnecessary minutia.

After the chair of the meeting has reviewed and approved the draft minutes, they should be distributed to all board or committee members for review prior to the next meeting. This is often sent as part of the pre-meeting packet. The board or committee should vote to approve the minutes at its next meeting.

Retention of meeting minutes

Additionally, the organization should retain its board meeting minutes permanently or a period consistent with the organization's document retention and destruction policy, as well as funder, government, and IRS regulations.

To facilitate board member effectiveness, consider storing all board minutes with a password protected online file hosting service and providing board members with a link to the folder. This will also enable them to review meeting minutes from any year. Information on several file-hosting services is provided in appendix B.

Board Minutes
October 15, 2014

Attendance
Present: Jane Doe, John Johnson, Jennifer Lane, Jane Smith, Steve Zeta. Absent: Jim Williams

Approval of Minutes
Motion was made to approve the September 17, 2014 board meeting minutes with one correction: Steve Zeta was present.

Motion: J. Johnson	Second: S. Zeta
Yes: 5	No: 0

Finance Committee Report
The Treasurer presented the 9/30/2014 YTD financials, which included $347,258 revenue and $343,273 expenses. After a short discussion, motion to accept the finance report was presented.

Motion: By the committee	Second: J. Williams
Yes: 5	No: 0

The Treasurer presented the FY 2015 budget for discussion and vote. The budget includes $465,000 of income and $451,435 of expense. Motion was made to approve the budget as presented.

Motion: By the committee	Second: J. Smith
Yes: 4	No: 1

Program Committee Report
The fundraising committee reported on the fall campaign, noting that board solicitations are essential to reaching the goal.

Human Resources Committee Report
Motion was made to increase the number of PTO days from 20 to 23.

Motion: By the committee	Second: J. Doe
Yes: 5	No: 0

STEP 6

Support Board Fundraising

Preparing board members for fundraising

The vast majority of board members are not professional fundraisers, and many have never actively volunteered as fundraisers. For this reason, board members need the right tools and support to successfully raise funds for the organization.

Each nonprofit organization is responsible for providing the following tools to its board members.

- An individual fundraising template to help structure a board member's fundraising activities
- Specific fundraising opportunities
- Appropriate solicitation materials
- Coaching and support
- Regular updates and reminders

The first step in helping board members fundraise is to provide an individual fundraising template. Typically distributed at the first meeting of the year, this template helps board members structure the fundraising activities they will engage in that year.

An effective template will ask board members to designate their own personal giving level, specific fundraising events they will promote through ticket sales, personal solicitations they will make, and other fundraising activities they will undertake.

A sample fundraising plan template follows on the next two pages. This is a sample, and each organization will need to customize its own.

Board Member Annual Fundraising Plan

Each Board member agrees to "give or get" at least $1,500 per year. So that we can best support your fundraising efforts, please complete the attached fundraising plan and return it to [Board or Fundraising Committee Chair]. As you complete this plan, keep in mind that your most effective fundraising efforts will come from soliciting family, friends, and colleagues. Feel free to attach additional paper if necessary.

My Personal Gift

My personal giving this year will total $_____ made by:

      ❑ Credit Card   ❑ Check   ❑ Securities.

I will give ❑ Monthly   ❑ Quarterly   ❑ Annually

      ❑ My employer will match this gift!

Major donor solicitations ($1,000 +)

I will solicit the following people for $1,000 or more:

_____

_____

_____

Special Events

I will solicit the following companies for a corporate gift or special event sponsorship:

Company   Amount

_____   _____

_____   _____

_____   _____

I will sell or purchase tickets to the following events:

Event Name	Ticket Cost	# Tickets	Total to be Raised
Annual Gala	$150	_____	$ _____
Tour of Homes	$35	_____	$ _____
Golf Tournament	$250	_____	$ _____

I will host a house party or other event:

Date:_____   Ticket Price: $_____

Number of Guests:_____   Total to be Raised: $_____

Relationships

I will cultivate the following individual, corporate, or organizational relationships.

_____

_____

_____

Annual Campaign

I will support the annual campaign by mailing personalized solicitation letters to (#)_____ of my friends. I plan to raise $_____ from this effort.

I will support the annual campaign by calling _____ lapsed donors and asking them to renew. I plan to raise $_____ from this effort.

Religious Support

I will ask my congregation or denomination to provide financial support to the organization and anticipate obtaining a contribution of $_____.

In-Kind

I will solicit in-kind contributions to offset items in the current year's budget.

Budget Item	Prospective Donor	Value
_____	_____	$_____
_____	_____	$_____
_____	_____	$_____

Board Member _____   _____
                           Signature   _Date_

Board Chair   _____   _____
                           Signature   _Date_

Helping board members identify prospective donors

When discussing the subject of board fundraising, board members often respond, "I would be happy to fundraise, but I really don't know anybody." For the most part, these board members just need a little help brainstorming the people they know who would support the mission of the organization. The simple tool below will help board members identify potential prospects in less than 10 minutes.

Brainstorm for Prospective Donors

In the space below, write the name of people you know who care about the mission of this organization.

From work:
_____
_____
_____

From college:
_____
_____
_____

Through my spouse:
_____
_____
_____

From civic organizations:
_____
_____
_____

In my family:
_____
_____
_____

From church/synagogue:
_____
_____
_____

In my neighborhood
_____
_____
_____

Miscellaneous
_____
_____
_____

Specific fundraising opportunities

Individual board members are responsible for fundraising, but most board members are not responsible for coordinating and planning specific fundraising events and campaigns.

For board members to successfully fulfill their fundraising obligations, the development committee and/or staff need to provide appropriate support. The following fundraising structures are most helpful to board members:

Special Events Existing special events are an excellent fundraising opportunity for board members. Since the event committee or staff handles all event logistics and marketing, board members can focus their energies on selling tickets, soliciting corporate sponsorship, and asking for general event donations.

The organization can support board members in selling tickets by providing them with invitations to send to friends. To make this even more effective, the organization can provide sample personal notes for members to write on the invitations they send. The organization will also need a system to track ticket purchases attributable to each board member's solicitation. This may be as simple as writing the board member's initials in the corner of an event reply card or assigning a link with a unique code to each board member for online ticket sales.

Additionally, board members may solicit their employers or other companies for sponsorships, and the organization will need to provide printed and digital copies of the sponsorship package. The appropriate staff person should coordinate solicitations to ensure no company is solicited by more than one person, and a suitably experienced staff person should join board members for meetings with prospective sponsors.

Annual Appeal Board members can personally solicit friends to support the organization through the annual appeal, typically conducted in the fall or spring. The fundraising staff will create solicitation letters, marketing collateral, and thank you letters that can support board involvement.

For board members who wish to solicit small gifts (typically of $250 or less), the organization can provide sample letters for board members to customize and send to their friends. You will increase your positive response rate if the solicitation letters direct donors to mail the response card and gift back to the board member. Since the member will know whether their friend has replied, the friend is more likely to make a donation. Peer pressure and the desire for social acceptance are powerful forces that will drive many to respond. The board member then bundles all gifts and delivers them to the organization.

Some board members will have friends committed to the mission who they want to solicit for a major gift. These solicitations should occur face-to-face. Ideally, the board member and executive director should begin the solicitation by offering tour of a facility or program. Prior to this tour, the executive director and board member should agree on which of them will actually ask for the gift and the amount to solicit.

Whether soliciting gifts in person or via mail, the board member should communicate their passion for the organization and enthusiasm for its programs. No solicitation technique more effectively closes a gift than a passionate board member asking for the donation.

House Parties Individual board members can host a house party with a suggested donation to attend and a short presentation during the party. Often, board members host such parties to coincide with birthdays, holidays, or special events (such as the Super Bowl or a local festival). Without a doubt, this is the most cost-effective way for an organization to grow its base of donors and supporters.

For all house parties, organization staff members are responsible for coordinating a short program and collateral materials for all guests, both of which ideally include client testimonials. Staff is also responsible for producing and sending timely written acknowledgement letters for of all donations made. The host typically manages all other logistics and pays party expenses.

Timely staff follow-up

Most important, the organization must ensure that people giving in response to a board solicitation have an excellent donor experience. At a minimum, the organization is responsible for sending timely written acknowledgements of ticket purchases or donations and follow-up thank you letters after events. Staff must also ensure that board members know when solicited gifts are actually received. Timeliness on both counts is critical to the board member's reputation because he or she has personally solicited the donation.

Recognizing board achievement

The organization should recognize board fundraising success both individually and as a governing body.

The board can celebrate individual fundraising efforts at each meeting. If a board member sold more gala tickets than anyone else, be sure to recognize the member and ask her to share a few tips about selling gala tickets. If a board member had a successful house party since the last meeting, ask him to tell the rest of the board about it.

Additionally, each board member should receive periodic individual fundraising updates that detail funds they have raised through specific campaigns or events. Staff can prepare this report before each meeting while compiling the aggregated data for the board member status reports. The fundraising update report will not only inform members of how much they have raised to date, but also gently remind them of their goal. An example status update is provided below, which can be added to the Board Expectation Report discussed in Chapter 2:

After producing the data for this report, the staff member responsible for fundraising should carefully check each of the figures in every board member's report. Additionally, the executive director should review them and write notes of encouragement or thanks to each member.

If a report indicates that a board member is at risk of not meeting his or her goal, the executive director, board chair, or fundraising chair should call that board member to ask about and suggest ways the organization can assist in meeting the goal.

The organization should also recognize the board's group achievements in fundraising. After achieving a major fundraising milestone, for example, a board officer or executive director can throw a cocktail party at his or her home to celebrate the success. It doesn't have to be a catered event at luxurious home, but guests should feel the party is festive, fun, and completely unlike a board meeting.

STEP 7

Offer Training to the Board

With the board evaluation complete, the board can also begin to consider training it needs as a body, as well as training that individual board members can consider to become more effective.

Board members most often need training in one or more of the following areas:

- Reading and understanding financial statements
- Fundraising tactics for board members
- Understanding and fulfilling their legal responsibilities
- Managing appropriate relationships with staff
- Understanding the organization's programs

Since each of these topics is covered in this book, this chapter will primarily focus on ways to consistently and appropriately deliver training. Because board members will have a variety of learning styles, it is important to offer a number of different types of training opportunities.

<u>Organic Training</u>: Some of the best training occurs organically, so that board members don't actually recognize it as "training." As an example, a treasurer could share a new tip for reviewing financials each time she presents the YTD financials at board meetings. At the January meeting, she might point out that the net YTD income is the same as the change in net assets on the balance sheet and briefly explain why they are the same. If a

board meets monthly, the treasurer will have taught the board twelve important facets of reviewing financial statements over the course of the year.

Brief Training Segments: Some boards dedicate ten or fifteen minutes in every meeting to board education. The training segment at one meeting might focus on how to solicit a major gift, and at another meeting might address appropriate relationships with staff. Training should typically be provided by previous board members with expertise in the specific topic or by someone else from outside of the organization.

Retreats: Many boards have an annual retreat to review the strategic plan and to bond as a group. This is a great opportunity to arrange for training on area(s) that were identified in your evaluation as being most critical for board development.

Orientation: Covered later in this book, the orientation of new board members is another opportunity to train board members about the agency's programs, history, and expectations of service.

Offsite Seminar: If your board evaluation asked members to identify areas in which they would like more training, those board members should be encouraged to register for an upcoming seminar in that area. Most local nonprofit resource centers offer low- or no-cost training that board members can attend.

STEP 8

Develop a Healthy Relationship With the Executive Director / CEO

upercharged boards enjoy a strong partnership with the executive director, and this partnership is essential for all successful nonprofits. These boards foster an open, honest, and trusting relationship with the executive director, who is included as a genuine partner in the work of the board. They also trust the executive director to competently manage operations, hire and supervise staff, and make good operational decisions.

Understanding the relationship between the board and the executive director is essential to achieving a supercharged board and having an effective organization. Unfortunately, an inappropriate relationship between the executive director and the board (or individual board members) is probably the most common cause of a dysfunctional nonprofit. The following pages outline appropriate roles for the board and executive director.

Hiring the executive director

The board is responsible for hiring the executive director, and every board member should take part in this process.

A 2014 LinkedIn discussion group posed the question of who should interview executive director candidates if only one board member was available for the interviews. Nearly every response agreed that selecting an executive director is one of the most important jobs of the board and, if members cannot make themselves available for the interviews, then they should not serve on the board.

While interviewing candidates may be delegated to a Board committee and structuring the search may be outsourced to a search firm, the board as a whole should discuss and approve the search structure. For the purposes of obtaining board approval, the search structure includes (at a minimum):

- The search firm or consultant to be retained, if any
- The executive director job description
- The pay scale for the position
- The plan for marketing the open position
- The interview process
- The search committee members
- The criteria for selecting the next executive director

Of course, the full board must also vote to hire the executive director, as well as set the maximum compensation the search committee is authorized to offer.

Evaluating the executive director

The board is also responsible for evaluating the executive director at least annually, and this is one of the most often-neglected board responsibilities. Typically, the executive director evaluation assesses performance in the areas of finances, regulatory and legal compliance, human resources, programs, and fundraising.

The board may choose to evaluate the executive director on other criteria, which should be clearly defined and communicated to the executive director at the beginning of the evaluation period.

Compensating the executive director

The board sets the executive director's salary and other compensation at the time of hire, but is also responsible for reviewing compensation at least annually, providing cost of living adjustments or other increases as it feels is appropriate.

Too many executive directors, with a deep commitment to the mission, fail to receive a salary increase after years of dedicated service. These executive directors often become resentful as inflation erodes the buying power of their compensation package, and they are torn between commitment to the organization and their own financial wellbeing.

Executive director's role in board meetings

The executive director should take part in all board meetings to serve as a resource, answer questions, and help provide an organizational perspective during discussions. Additionally, participation in meetings allows the executive director to better understand the intent of each motion and manage the organization in a manner consistent with the board's wishes.

For this reason, there are only four occasions when the board should exclude the executive director:

- When discussing the executive director's annual evaluation
- When discussing the executive director's compensation
- When discussing the possibility of disciplining or terminating the executive director
- When investigating reported illegal or unethical behavior of the executive director

To preserve trust, the board should inform the executive director prior to scheduling such a meeting. In doing so, they should clearly communicate the reason for the closed meeting and provide a timeline for next steps following the meeting.

Most important, supercharged boards always inform an executive director if closed meetings will occur before the director learns of the meeting from a staff member, community member, or the "rumor mill". Learning of the meeting from a source other than the board will immediately undermine the executive director's trust in the board and ability to manage the organization. At that point, the relationship is most likely irreparable.

Who does what?

In addition to the responsibilities outlined in previous chapters, the board is responsible for setting the strategic direction and approving organizational policies. The executive director is responsible for implementing those policies and running the organization. The executive director's responsibilities include (a) negotiating and executing contracts; (b) hiring, managing, and terminating staff; (c) making decisions essential to the regular operations of the organization.

It is important to understand that individual board members and officers are just individual board members. As such, a board member or officer lacks the authority to supervise the executive director or create policy. Only the full board, in a legally recognized meeting, has the authority to engage in these activities.

Regardless of serving as a committee member or even as a committee chair, a board member is never responsible for directly managing a program, implementing policy decisions, managing staff, mediating among staff, or making employment decisions. These remain key staff functions, and board members who attempt to make such decisions cause role confusion for all staff, the board, and the clients served.

As stated in chapter 6, boards that engage in such behavior undermine the effectiveness of the organization, leaving the staff leader without the credibility to manage staff, collaborate with organization partners, or work with funders.

STEP 9

Recruit the Right Members

I f your board has completed the steps in each of the other chapters, you are ready to launch a robust and successful recruitment campaign. While the nominating committee is tasked with overseeing recruitment and orientation, a successful recruitment campaign requires the support and work of the entire board. The steps of successful recruitment campaigns are:

- Identify all the skills and connections the board needs to function effectively
- Identify those skills and connections not currently represented among board members
- Develop an application for prospective board members
- Structure a robust campaign to recruit board members
- Create a system for carefully considering each candidate
- Recommend the best candidates for board appointment
- Follow up with all candidates not appointed to the board and connect them with volunteer opportunities

So that the nominating committee can easily identify skills and connections most needed at the start of the annual recruitment cycle, the committee should begin by creating a list of all the skills and connections the board needs to function well, including those met by present board members. Each organization will have a different list but a minimum list includes expertise in:

- Accounting
- Fundraising
- Governance
- Human resources
- Legal and regulatory matters
- Marketing
- Program evaluation
- Program subject matter
- Public relations and/or media relations
- Volunteer fundraising

The nominating committee should also create a list of needed connections, which may include:

- Local government
- State government
- Federal agency
- Area corporations and businesses
- Media and entertainment
- Faith communities
- Ethnic and minority communities

The nominating committee can expand the list or add more detail based on the organization's complexity.

An organization with an annual fundraising 5K race, for example, may want at least one board member with expertise in coordinating race events, and at least one board member with strong connections among running groups. Another organization whose mission is to build wheel chair ramps for disabled adults would likely want someone with expertise in construction and a board member with strong connections at the municipal planning department.

Once the nominating committee has developed a list of needed skills and connections, it can create a board matrix. The matrix for a fictional adult training agency may look something like the one provided on the following two pages.

	Member #1	Member #2	Member #3	Member #4	Member #5	Member #6	Member #7	
Term Ends	2015	2015	2016	2016	2017	2017	2017	
Eligible for 2nd term?	Y	N	Y	N	N	Y	Y	Count
Expertise								
Finance and accounting								0
Fundraising—individuals	X							1
Fundraising—events			X					1
Governance						X		1
Workforce development						X		1
Adult education							X	1
Human resources								0
Information technology			X					1
Leadership development					X			1
Law								0
Marketing					X			1
Media relations								0
Meeting procedures	X			X				2
Strategic planning			X			X		2
Program evaluation				X				1

	Member #1	Member #2	Member #3	Member #4	Member #5	Member #6	Member #7	
Term Ends	2015	2015	2016	2016	2017	2017	2017	
Eligible for 2nd term?	Y	N	Y	N	N	Y	Y	Count
Connections								
Local WFD agency								0
GA Dept of Labor	X							0
Foundations								0
Area corporations			X			X		2
Communities of faith		X		X		X		3
Organized labor								0
Cultural organizations								0
African American communities		X	X					1
Asian communities								0
Latino communities					X			1
Elders								0
Young adults								0
Rural/suburban communities		X				X		2
Media outlets								0
Entertainment Industry					X			1

Reviewing the board matrix for this fictional organization, this board needs members with accounting, human resources, legal, and media skills. It also needs board members that have connections with the local workforce development agency (WFD), foundations, organized labor, cultural organizations, Asian communities, young adults, elders, and media outlets.

With this knowledge, the Nominating Committee can create a robust recruitment campaign that targets people with these skills and connections.

Develop a board application

Each nominating committee should carefully structure its own application to obtain sufficient information for interviewing candidates and checking their backgrounds. For this reason, it is critically important for each prospective board member to complete an application.

Additionally, being on a board is a great deal of work, and taking the time to complete an application indicates a willingness to do the work necessary. A candidate who never completes an application is very likely to become a board member who does not read meeting packets, complete organizational documents, or follow through on commitments.

A sample application follows, and nominating committees should edit this application to meet their own needs.

Sample Application for Board Membership

Thank you for your interest in serving on the XYZ Organization Board of Directors. Please complete the attached application and return it to nominations@freshstartinit.org by March 31, 2015. Nominating interviews will take place the week of March 30 with new board members beginning their first term on July 1, 2015. New Board member orientation is scheduled for Saturday July 11.

_____ _____ _____
First Name   MI   Last Name

_____
Street Address

_____ _____ _____
City   State   ZIP

_____ _____
Phone Number   Alternate Phone

_____
Email Address

_____
Occupation and place of business

_____ _____
Years at current job   Date of Birth

How did you first learn about the organization?

Why do you want to serve on this board?

Which of the following areas of expertise will you bring to board service?
❑ Legal   ❑ Accounting   ❑ Media Relations   ❑ Board Governance
❑ Marketing   ❑ Advocacy   ❑ Program Area(s)   ❑ Program Client
❑ Professional Fundraiser   ❑ Volunteer Fundraiser

What other skills or experiences will you bring to board service? If you indicated program area expertise above, please describe.

Please list the degrees you have received, including school and year of graduation:

If you have served on a nonprofit board before, please provide the organization name, dates or service, and reason for leaving, for up to three most recent board position(s):

Do we have your permission to contact the organizations listed above about your board service?

❑ Yes   ❑ No   ❑ Not Applicable

We conduct a criminal background investigation on all board candidates. Are you willing to sign a release allowing us to conduct the investigation?

❑ Yes   ❑ No

What is your general availability for board and committee meetings? Please specify days or times that you are unable to participate in meetings:

Please check the evenings you are available for an interview with the nominating committee:

❑ March 30   ❑ March 31   ❑ April 1   ❑ April 4

Board Meetings are scheduled for the third Monday each month from 6:30 P.M. to 8:30 P.M. Are you usually available at this time?

❑ Yes   ❑ No

The minimum expectations for board members are listed below. Please confirm your ability and willingness to meet these by initialing each expectation.

If selected for the board:

_____ I will attend and actively participate in at least 10 of the 12 monthly board meetings.

_____ I will make a personal annual financial gift at a level that is personally significant.

_____ I will raise at least $500 per year for the organization by direct solicitations, selling tickets to events, or other fundraising activities.

_____ I will serve on at least one committee and attending at least 10 of the committee's 12 monthly meetings.

_____ I will will manage at least three relationships on behalf of the organization.

Please sign your application, attach your resume, and return it to **email@email.com** or fax it to (404) 555-5555.

_____   _____

Signature   *Date*

Structure a robust board recruitment campaign

The nominating committee is responsible for structuring a robust board recruitment campaign. As stated in chapter 6, a board will function more efficiently if there is one recruitment campaign annually. This allows all new board members to start at the same time and receive orientation as a group.

The nominating committee's next step is drafting a board recruitment announcement. A good announcement:

- States the name and mission of the organization
- Identifies the skills and connections most needed
- Outlines the requirements of board service
- Informs readers how to apply for board service

The nominating committee will use this announcement throughout its outreach efforts to individuals and organizations.

Next the committee needs to determine the specific individuals and organizations to approach about board service.

In considering individuals to approach, the nominating committee should review the following reports from development staff:

- Major donors
- Donors who have regularly given small amounts to the organization over many years
- Organization volunteers

The nominating committee should review each of these lists to consider which individuals might provide some of the skills and connections most needed by the board. The executive director and committee chairs will be invaluable in providing information about individuals on these lists before the nominating committee contacts them.

Additionally, the nominating committee should brainstorm professional associations, corporate volunteer departments and other outlets available to market the open board positions. This might include:

- The local bar association
- The local chapter of the Society for Human Resource Management
- The local chapter of the American Institute for CPAs or National Society of Accountants
- The local board-training program (often run by United Way, community foundation, or nonprofit resource center)
- Local chapter of the Public Relations Society of America
- Community involvement programs of large professional firms providing accounting, marketing, public relations, or other consulting services
- Premium LinkedIn account, which allows a committee member to search appropriate professionals seeking board membership.

After narrowing the list to two or three dozen prospects, the nominating committee should divide the list among itself and personally contact each candidate. The nominating chair should email members to ask for an update in one week and follow-up by phone with those that do not respond.

Finally, the nominating committee chair should email all board members to ask for nomination recommendations and personally follow up with anyone recommended.

The nominating committee should have a member identified who will send an application promptly to those who express an interest in applying for board service. One week before the application deadline, the committee should provide a courtesy follow-up phone call to those who received applications. Once again, the nominating committee may wish to share the burden of making these calls.

Reviewing applicants

Most board chairs would agree that the best and worst board decisions have been the people appointed to the board. For this reason, the nominating committee should exercise due diligence in reviewing, interviewing, and recommending prospective board members.

The nominating committee should meet in person for the sole purpose of reviewing applications, and the committee should pay close attention to the following:

- How applicants' skills align with the board's skill gaps
- For applicants with previous board service, whether they completed their full terms and why they left the board
- Why applicants are interested in serving on your board
- Whether applicants are willing and able to meet the board expectations

As a general rule, the Nominating Committee should interview twice as many candidates as available board positions. If, for example, the goal is to fill four board vacancies, the committee should invite at least eight candidates for interview. Some candidates will decline the opportunity to interview, others will remove themselves from the process after the interview, and the committee may strike some candidates as a result of the interview.

If a particular committee member reached out to an individual during the recruitment and application process, the same committee member should schedule the interview.

Prior to the interview, a member of the nominating committee should conduct reference checks on each selected candidate. At a minimum, this includes calling the executive director and board chair of organizations on whose boards the candidate has previously served and asking the following questions:

- What dates did the board member serve?
- What were the person's greatest contributions as a board member?
- What skills did this person bring to the board?
- What challenges did this person bring to the board?
- Why and how did board service end?
- Would you have them on your board again?

If the executive director or board president offers a different answer from that listed on the candidate's application, the committee should diplomatically inquire about this when interviewing the candidate. A significantly different response is a red flag, however reasonable the candidate's explanation for the discrepancy sounds. Dig deeper and proceed cautiously with such a candidate, as your goal is to "hire" productive board members.

It is better to reject a potentially great board member than to appoint a poison apple to your board.

Interview board candidates

Interviewing board candidates is the final critical step of reviewing board applications, and this is the last opportunity to determine who will be the best candidate (and the last opportunity to weed out bomb throwers).

Choose a private, confidential setting for the interviews. Ideally, interviews are held in the conference room where the board actually meets. If the organization does not have a private conference room, interviews can be conducted in a conference room at a committee member's office.

When interviewing the prospective board members be certain to ask about:

- Any discrepancies between the responses on their application and the responses of their references
- Which accomplishments give them the greatest pride, particularly achievements made in board service to another organization
- The reason(s) they want to serve on this board, instead of an organization with a similar mission
- The reasons they have or have not donated to the organization in the past
- Any issues that may prevent them from meeting the expectations of board service or serving their full terms
- Confirmation that they can meet each of the board expectations
- Confirmation that the day and time of board meetings is convenient for them.

Recommending candidates for board appointment

The nominating committee is responsible for recommending candidates for board appointments and needs to give the board the opportunity to consider each candidate. For this reason, the committee should recommend specific candidates and provide their applications, resumes, and a written summary of the reasons for each recommendation.

Following up with every board candidate

After the board has voted to fill current and anticipated vacancies, the nominating committee should follow up with each candidate personally.

Follow up with those appointed to the board: Initially, the board chair should call those appointed to the board within two business days of the board meeting. The call should congratulate them and clearly communicate a sense of excitement about their board service.

Calls should end with a reminder of the board orientation date and inform candidates that they will receive a welcome package by mail. The board chair should let the executive director know once he or she has spoken with each incoming board member, so that the executive director can also make congratulatory calls and ensure each new member receives the welcome package.

Follow up with those interviewed but not appointed to the board: The nominating committee chair should call each candidate within two business days of the board meeting. An outline for the nominating committee chair's conversation with those not being appointed follows:

- Thank the candidate for applying.
- Indicate the board faced a difficult decision with many well-qualified candidates.
- Share that they were not selected for board service this year.

- Invite the candidate to serve on a specific committee. Demonstrate sincerity of the request by naming contributions the chair feels the candidate would make in such a role.
- Let them know that a staff member will follow up with them about committee service.
- Thank them again for applying and their support of the organization.

Once the nominating committee chair has completed the call, the executive director should call the candidate and also thank them for participating in the process. If the candidate is interested in committee service, the executive director can share the next steps in beginning volunteer service during this call.

Often candidates not selected for the board ask for feedback about why they were not selected. It is best to be honest but kind in following up with the candidate.

How you form your response depends on whether the board might seriously consider the candidate for membership in the future. For example, if the committee selected someone else because the successful candidate's skills or connections better fit the board's needs, say that the other accountant (for example) had a specific attribute that the board really needs right now. If the board had more personal misgivings, address those honestly but compassionately and without going into detail.

Those not interviewed by the nominating committee

Each person who submitted an application but was not interviewed for the board should receive a brief and courteous letter thanking them for applying and letting them know other candidates have been selected for the board. This letter is typically signed by the nominating committee chair but prepared and mailed by staff.

Communicating this by letter instead of email is preferred for two reasons. First, the rejected candidate is less likely to write back requesting more details about why they were not selected. Second, a small percentage of these candidates may forward an email to others and include disparaging remarks about the organization.

If the applicant not interviewed happens to be a donor or volunteer, more personal follow-up is warranted. This may include a personal call from the executive director thanking them for their interest and sharing that many highly qualified people applied for board service.

STEP 10

Orient New Board Members

Effective board orientation ensures that board members start their tenure with sufficient information to competently serve in a leadership position. For this reason, all freshmen board members should complete the board orientation before attending an actual board meeting.

Board officers should facilitate the orientation, and the executive director should be included to ensure he or she continues to build relationships with the freshmen board members.

Topics included in board orientation

Boards that have approved policies and procedures as outlined in each of the preceding chapters will have many of the written materials needed for a robust and relevant orientation, which includes:

History: Provide a brief overview of the organization's history and important milestones. This is a good time to provide collateral materials such as brochures, newsletters, and annual reports. The executive director can showcase his or her storytelling prowess by facilitating this section.

Expectations: Even though board expectations are clearly outlined during the recruitment process, the orientation should reiterate each of the expectations. The board chair is the best person to facilitate this, and this is a good opportunity to have freshmen board members complete the conflict of interest disclosure and board expectations documents (see chapter 2).

Rules of Engagement: Covering the board-approved rules of engagement at orientation prepares board members to adhere to them. In outlining the rules of engagement, be certain to explain the process the board used to develop them, as well as how the rules of engagement help the board function more effectively. This is a good opportunity for the board vice chair to facilitate.

Financials: Review the most recent YTD financials, audited financials, and IRS form 990. The treasurer should facilitate this review and answer questions freshmen board members may have.

Legal Documents and Meetings: Provide copies and explain the highlights of the organization's bylaws, articles of incorporation, and minutes from the prior year. Providing minutes from the prior year ensures that board members have a historical context of current business.

Additionally, freshmen should receive a schedule of all board meetings including date, time, location, and teleconference options. The board secretary may facilitate this section.

Fundraising: Provide details about the organization's fundraising campaigns and events. Be certain to indicate how individual board members participate in and support these efforts. Include a list of all fundraising events and campaigns currently scheduled, as well as a list of the top five or ten funders. Following this section, freshmen board members should complete their individualized board fundraising templates (see Step 4).

Committee Structure: Freshmen board members should learn about the committee structure, as well as the annual work plan and meeting schedule of each committee. Freshmen members should also have the opportunity to request a specific committee appointment, and many organizations will have started the committee appointment discussion as part of recruitment. This section should also include a discussion of board roles and responsibilities as compared to staff roles and responsibilities.

Programs: In addition to general program information, you should provide specific descriptions and outcome information for each program. This is a great opportunity for the program committee chair or staff program director to present and also an opportunity to have a client share their personal testimonial.

Strategic Plan: Since the strategic plan guides the development of the organization over a several year period, the board chair can outline the plan's most important components. If a new strategic planning process will occur during the new members' tenure, this should also be mentioned.

Organizational chart: The executive director can present the organizational chart and explain the roles of key staff members.

Facilities: If the organization operates facility-based programs, the orientation should include a facility tour and discussion of any outstanding facility needs or planned improvements.

Scheduling

The board should hold orientation before freshmen members attend their first meeting, and board candidates should be informed of the orientation date when they submit applications. The orientation will likely require six to eight hours, which includes time for ice breakers, a group meal, and breaks.

Make the orientation engaging

It is important to make the orientation as engaging as possible; after all no one wants to sit through an eight-hour lecture. A few ideas for making the orientation more engaging include:

- Schedule a client testimonial every 90 minutes.
- Have a 30-minute break out session where board members develop their 90-second "elevator speech" about why they love the organization and then present these to the group.
- Give nominal awards for those who exhibit exemplary volunteerism (such as the first to volunteer to introduce themselves, volunteer for a committee, or turn in their conflict of interest form).
- A facilitator can present one of the sections in song or metric verse. (This requires a lot of advance work, but is tremendous fun at the event.)

If these ideas don't seem engaging for your board's orientation, find your own unique ways to make the orientation more fun and authentic to you and your organization!

Orientation doesn't stop after the first month

The first orientation session prepares board members for their first meeting, but truly learning how to be a good board member takes time and practice. For this reason, the additional orientation strategies detailed below will reinforce the information provided in the initial orientation session.

Recruit and Assign Mentors. Each freshmen board member should be assigned a current board member as mentor. The mentor should be a stellar, high-achieving board member who exudes enthusiasm for the organization, meets expectations, and follows the rules of engagement. The mentor should:

- Celebrate the mentee's successes. Example: A short email thanking the board member for bringing four people to a fundraising event.
- Make serving on the board a more social experience. Example: Ask the mentee for coffee or drinks after a board meeting.

- Recognize milestones in the mentee's life or career. Example: Make a small gift to the organization in their honor when they receive a big promotion.
- Reinforce board expectations. Example: Offer to co-host a house party with a mentee who is having difficulty meeting fundraising expectations.

<u>Recognize Board Members' Successes</u>. At each board meeting, be certain to take a few minutes to recognize all board members who have achieved significant success. This will help reinforce the orientation and clearly indicate that freshmen board members' successes will also be recognized. A few examples include:

- Pass around a tablet with digital photos of a board member's successful house party.
- Offer a champagne toast to a finance committee member that worked extra hard to help resolve a difficult financial issue (at the close of the meeting, of course).
- Print a newsletter feature story about a program committee that played a leadership volunteer role in merging two programs, providing better services at a lower cost. Be sure to pass out the newsletter at the board meeting and highlight the committee's success.
- Give the human resources committee a standing ovation for working with legal counsel to recommend excellent revisions to the HR manual.
- Host a board holiday party where exemplary achievements are recognized.

If none of these suggestions are appropriate for recognizing your board's achievement, a simple web search will suggest many more ideas for you to consider.

Enforce Expectations

Freshmen board members benefit from seeing the board enforce its own expectations. If a board member goes on a leave of absence after missing too many meetings, for example, then the newer board members learn that this expectation is enforced. Enforcing expectations helps set the norm for new board members.

Putting It All Together

After reading and understanding the material in this book, you have the tools necessary to supercharge your board. Whether you are the executive director, the board chair, or a board member, it is now time to take the first step by presenting the system outlined in this book to the appropriate committee or board for consideration.

As your organization works through each step of the process, you will undoubtedly encounter impediments, distractions, and even naysayers. Do not let these short term obstacles distract from the important work your board must undertake to be fully supercharged.

To assist you in this process, I have made all of the book's templates available as modifiable MS Word documents. If you would like to download the documents for your nonprofit's use, visit www.goldenburggroup.com. The password to download documents found in this book is *1-2-3-Supercharge!* (password includes the exclamation point).

If you fully implement each step, your organization can have a highly engaged, supercharged board that understands its obligations, fulfills its oversight responsibilities, follows through on commitments, and serves as the organization's most persuasive fundraisers and ambassadors.

Appendix A: Sample Board Manual Table of Contents

As part of orientation, each organization should provide its board with a manual, either in paper or electronic format. The typical board manual includes:

<u>Founding Documents</u>:

    Articles of Incorporation

    Bylaws

    IRS issued 501(c)(3) determination letter

    Annual nonprofit registration certificate (if required by the relevant jurisdiction's Secretary of State)

<u>Board Information</u>:

    Board member expectations document

    Conflict of interest policy

    Annual board and committee calendar

    Committee descriptions

    Board member and officer job descriptions

    Board roster, with contact information

    Minutes from prior year's board meetings

    Information about any technology that board members need to fulfill their duties

    All documents and forms board members complete annually

Financial Information:

    Current fiscal year budget, with narrative and comparison to prior fiscal year

    Most recent audited financial statements (most recent)

    Unaudited YTD financial statements (most recent)

    IRS form 990 (most recent)

    Financial policies manual

Organization Information:

    Strategic plan

    Strategic plan progress report (most recent)

    History of organization

    Description of programs and services

    Program output and outcome data

    Annual report

    Organizational chart

    Employee manual

Fundraising and Marketing:

    Marketing materials (such as newsletters or brochures)

    Annual fundraising plan

    Description of all fundraising activities from prior year, including gross and net revenue

Appendix B: Technology Resources to Supercharge Your Board

Supercharged boards use technology to communicate more effectively, plan with greater ease, and enable retention and easy access to board documents. Typically, staff is responsible for setting up the technology systems, and may need to train some board members in how to use them.

Each service listed below has unique features and different price structures. For this reason, give careful consideration to ensure the services selected meet the organization's need and budget. Caveat Emptor.

Communication

A number of services can provide online conference services, including the sharing of one or more desktops. Such services bridge board members into meetings they would otherwise miss and enable committees to meet remotely. Services to consider include:

www.gotomeeting.com
www.join.me
www.dozeo.com
www.clickmeeting.com
www.zoho.com

Planning

A simple online tool useful for scheduling meetings is www.doodle.com. These affordable tools are useful for project management:

www.asana.com

www.basecamp.com

Board document storage

Providing easily accessible board documents (such as upcoming meeting agendas, meeting minutes, and the board manual) enables board members to use their volunteer time on meaningful activities instead of meaningless filing. These sites offer excellent real-time online storage and syncing:

www.dropbox.com

www.google.com/drive

www.skydrive.com

www.box.com

Acknowledgements

This text is the culmination of knowledge gained from many years as a nonprofit CEO and board member. As an executive director, I have had the pleasure of working with many board chairs. While each board chair taught me important lessons outlined in this book, I owe a tremendous debt of thanks to several board chairs. They include Rhonda K.R. Cook, Raymond Becker, Deborah Francesco, and David Michelson.

Lori L. Jean taught me so much when we served together as board co-chairs of CenterLink, a national nonprofit serving LGBT community centers. Despite her incredibly busy schedule, she was always available when I would ask for a "mentoring moment".

Vanessa Kucera's expert editing shortened the original manuscript, enabling you to easily read the entire book on a Sunday afternoon.

Of course, my greatest thanks go to the love of my life, Frank Hartley. Whether I have a great day or a tough day, I always delight in seeing his smiling face at home that evening.

About the Author

D olph Ward Goldenburg is recognized as a high performance leader in the nonprofit sector.

Goldenburg serves as managing director of The Goldenburg Group, LLC, which provides organizational development, strategic planning, grant solutions, and interim executive services to nonprofit organizations.

As a successful CEO for 11 years, Goldenburg has a demonstrated history of leading nonprofit organizations to financial stability and growth. In his CEO roles, he has successfully turned deficits into surpluses, grown budgets and programs, and improved facilities.

In addition to extensive CEO experience, Goldenburg also has more than a decade of fundraising experience. He has solicited six-figure gifts, increased annual campaign revenue, and written millions of dollars in funded grant proposals.

Goldenburg also has significant experience as a nonprofit board member, including a successful term as board co-chair of the national nonprofit CenterLink.

Goldenburg has been recognized by the Pennsylvania Senate, received the Visionary of the Year Award from Visions Today Magazine, named Person of the Year by the Philadelphia Gay News, and identified as one of the 101 Most Connected Philadelphians by Leadership Philadelphia.

Visit www.goldenburggroup.com to learn more about Dolph Ward Goldenburg or The Goldenburg Group, LLC.

Made in the USA
Lexington, KY
22 May 2016